HOW TO
Start a Business
Step-by-Step Guide

By Violet James, MSM

Maximum Potential, LLC

HOW TO Start a Business
Step-by-Step Guide

By Violet James, MSM

advertising, and all other aspects of doing business in the United States or any other jurisdiction is the sole responsibility of the Purchaser or Reader. The Author and Publisher assume no responsibility or liability whatsoever on the behalf of any Purchaser or Reader of these materials.

HOW TO Start a Business Step-by-Step Guide is also available in eBook version for Kindle. You can download on your Kindle™ tablet, iPhone®, iPod®, and Android™. To download go to Amazon.com.

TABLE OF CONTENTS

Introduction

Congratulations!

You are on your way to starting your own business. At first you might feel a little overwhelmed by the amount of work that needs to get done, but don't worry I have broken down the process into manageable basic steps. So let's get started!

To your prosperous journey,

Violet James

"A journey of a thousand miles begins with a single step."
~Lao Tzu

Please note: This guide is a good starting point for you to begin a business. It is in no way meant to be a substitute for professional advice or counsel.

Step 1:

Brainstorming Session

What good is inspiration if it's not backed up by action? ~Tony Robbins

Make sure your idea is focused and clearly defined. Start with the purpose (mission) and the goals that you plan to accomplish.

Ask yourself the following questions:

1. What product or service will I offer?
2. Do I have the skills, interest and passion for this specific business idea/industry?
3. Do I have experience in this industry and am I willing to learn and do everything I can to get more?
4. Am I willing to commit to the long hours needed to make this business grow and succeed?
5. What will the startup costs be? How much money will I need to begin?

1

6. Is this idea something that can be profitable and cover costs? How long will it take to make a profit?

When you feel good about an idea then it's time to test it. You can hire a marketing research firm or do some research and testing on your own. Doing market research doesn't have to be complicated or expensive. You can test your product idea or service yourself. Just ask potential customers (friends, family, co-workers, etc) to give you constructive, honest feedback about your idea. Would they buy this product/service? How much are they willing to pay? What was their first impression of the idea? Try to get as much honest feedback as possible and listen intently. Try not to get discouraged and defensive with negative feedback, instead learn from it and make some improvements and changes, if needed.

Resources to help you find a profitable business idea:

Business Idea Center - 969 Businesses You Can Start Today *by Entrepreneur Magazine*
http://www.entrepreneur.com/businessideas

The Top 10 Small Business Bets, Post-Recession and Next Recession *by Entrepreneur Magazine*
http://www.entrepreneur.com/article/233491

Step 2:

Defining Your Business

The true entrepreneur is a doer, not a dreamer. ~ Nolan Bushnell

Brainstorm a business name that people will remember and that fits the image/branding that you would like to create for your new business. Check to see if your name is unique by doing searches on the internet (google/yahoo/bing). Once you select a name, you want to find out if the name is available and not already taken by another company. If it's not available, you will have to think of some other alternative names. Trade names can be registered at the state and federal levels. For the state level the trade name can be registered with the Secretary of State office and for broader protection it can be registered through the US Patent and Trademark Office (USPTO). So, check with your Secretary of State office and the USPTO to see if your proposed name is available or unavailable.

Secretary of State Databases – Find online searchable databases
http://www.coordinatedlegal.com/SecretaryOf
State.html

US Patent and Trademark Office (USPTO) – Find trademark information and searchable databases
http://www.uspto.gov/

In addition, you may want to check if a website domain name is available in the business name you are considering. You can conduct searches and register domain names at the following websites:

www.NameSecure.com
www.Register.com
www.NetworkSolutions.com
www.GoDaddy.com

Step 3:

What is the Plan?

Failing to prepare is like preparing to fail.
~Author Unknown

The next step is to prepare a business plan. Many people feel they do not need a business plan. However, if you will be seeking funding from a bank for a business loan or venture capitalists, then a detailed business plan is required for the application process. Even if you raise money from family and friends, you will still need to communicate your vision and goals confidently and clearly. A business plan is a well thought-out, strategic plan that outlines and defines what products/services you will be providing, your specific goals and objectives, operating procedures, competition, projected income and expenses as well as marketing strategies.

If you are inexperienced and uncomfortable creating your own business plan, you can hire a professional business consultant to work with you to complete it or you can get free assistance from a variety of nonprofit sources such as:

www.Score.org - They offer free mentoring, workshops and have SCORE local chapters you can join. 1-800-634-0245

www.sba.gov - US Small Business Administration – They offer counseling, mentoring, and training from an SBA District office. 1-800-827-5722

Local Assistance Tool SBA - Connect with your local SBA district office and other resources in your local area. https://www.sba.gov/tools/local-assistance

Step 4:

Making it Legal

Don't be upset with the results you didn't get with the work you didn't do.
~Author Unknown

For questions regarding legal set-up and requirements for your specific type of business, it is best to get advice from an attorney and/or accountant. You can also seek help from nonprofit organizations such as SCORE and the US Small Business Administration (see contact information in Step 3). In addition, you can establish a board of advisors or mentors/professionals to help you along the way.

The main steps that need to be completed to meet legal requirements to operate a business are as follows:

**Please note that these steps should not be construed as all-inclusive. Other steps may be needed for your specific type of business.

A. Protect Your Idea

If you created and designed your own product, process, logo, printed materials/manuals, etc you will want to get legal protection and speak with an attorney. Legal protection options include:

a. **Patent** – Protects an original product idea, new design or process. *Contact*: The United States Patent and Trademark Office - http://www.uspto.gov/ 1-800-786-9199

b. **Trademark –** Protects a product name, logo, design, slogan, symbol, etc. *Contact*: The United States Patent and Trademark Office

c. **Servicemark** – Protects a brand or service name, logo, design, symbol, etc. *Contact*: The United States Patent and Trademark Office

d. **Copyright** – Protects printed and audio material such as books, manuals, soundtracks, computer software, etc. *Contact:* The United States Copyright Office http://www.copyright.gov/ 1-877-476-0778

B. Choose a Formal Structure

You will need to decide what form of business entity to establish for legal and financial purposes. The business structure you have will determine what income tax forms you will need to file.

There are four main choices:
- Sole Proprietorship
- Partnership
- Corporation or S-Corporation
- Limited Liability Company (LLC)

Corporations and LLC's provide the owner with personal asset protection from debts and liabilities of the company. *Caution:* If you set up your business structure as a sole proprietor or partnership, you are personally liable for your business debt. Talk to an attorney or accountant for specifics.

For more information about each business structure, go to:

IRS Business Structures –
http://www.irs.gov/Businesses/Small-Businesses-&-Self-Employed/Business-Structures

US Small Business Administration -
Choose Your Business Structure
https://www.sba.gov/category/navigation-structure/starting-managing-business/starting-business/choose-your-business-stru

Once you decide on a legal structure for your new business then find your state requirements on how and what needs to be filed for your specific state *(You can type in google search for example-Filing a LLC in Michigan).*

**Please note: The process and steps are completely different for starting and filing for a nonprofit organization and are not covered in this guide.

C. Apply for an Employer Identification Number (EIN)

You will need to obtain a federal tax identification number (also called an Employer Identification Number or EIN). If your business structure is setup as a Corporation, LLC, or Partnership you are required to apply for an EIN from the IRS. If you are setup as a Sole Proprietorship then you only need this number if you plan on hiring employees. The EIN is used by the IRS to identify your business for all taxation matters and helps separate you from your business. It will also be necessary to have an EIN to open a business bank account or process payroll. EIN numbers are free and you can apply online. Go to:

IRS Apply for an EIN Online –
http://www.irs.gov/Businesses/Small-Businesses-&-Self-Employed/Employer-ID-Numbers-EINs

D. Obtain the Necessary Business Licenses and Permits

Most licenses and permits are at the state and/or local level. You may need to obtain the necessary business licenses and/or permits required by your city, municipality, county and/or state depending on your industry and where you are located. For example, if your company sells physical products within the state in does business, you may be required to file for a sales tax license. Contact your Secretary of State and local government to find out how to obtain the necessary licenses to ensure you meet the requirements. For more information go to:

SBA Obtain Business Licenses and Permits Tool
https://www.sba.gov/licenses-and-permits

IRS Specific State Requirements for Small Business – State Links
http://www.irs.gov/Businesses/Small-Businesses-&-Self-Employed/State-Links-1

E. Obtain Business Insurance

Depending on the type of business you are starting, you may need liability insurance (sometimes called General Business Insurance or Business Owner's Policy). This can offer an extra level of protection for your business. Another option is to have a Business Rider added to a homeowner's policy. If you have employees, you may also need workers compensation insurance and/or health insurance. Discuss your specific industry and business needs with an insurance agent to obtain the appropriate type and amount of insurance needed. Listed below are a few insurance companies that offer small business policies:

State Farm Insurance- Business Insurance
https://www.statefarm.com/small-business-solutions/insurance

Farmers Insurance- Small Business Insurance
http://www.farmers.com/business/

Step 5:

Financing Your Business

There is no security on the earth, there is only opportunity. ~General Douglas MacArthur

It can be more challenging in the start-up phase to secure funds and manage cash flow. However, it doesn't have to be if you are well prepared and have a solid business plan with projected financial costs/budgets.

A. Open a Business Checking Account/ Merchant Account

  a. Start with opening up a Business Checking Account. Most banks require an EIN to open a business account. This keeps your personal and business assets separate from each other. Many banks offer free business checking accounts with no minimum balances and monthly fees.

b. You may also need to open a Merchant Account (credit card processing) if you want to take credit cards as payment. Find merchant service companies and get several quotes to compare the processing fees for small businesses.

B. Obtain Credit

Obtaining credit and using it wisely as a money management tool can have many benefits such as: you can have working capital (money) for operating expenses, inventory, growth opportunities, and emergencies. Also, your business can establish a good credit history and you can start a good working relationship with your bank.

a. **Business Credit Card** – A card will help you establish a favorable credit history if paid on time. Use for purchases, supplies, travel and entertainment, etc. You have the option to pay your bills in full or revolve your balance.

b. **Business Check Card (Debit Card)** – This card can be used instead of cash and checks. The amount gets taken out of your business checking account.

c. **Business Line of Credit** – This is a line of credit to help businesses manage cash flow. You can have working capital for operating expenses, inventory, emergencies and growth opportunities. These loans are given by financial institutions (banks).

C. Obtain Financing/Funding

First, determine how much startup capital you will need. Create a financial startup budget. Keep in mind that you will need enough money to survive for at least six to eight months while your business is launching. Some small business owners do not have enough of their own capital to cover the startup costs. So, getting funds from other sources will be necessary.

a. **Own Investment, Family and Friends -** Some business owners will use their personal assets (capital) to fund the business or ask family and/or friends to invest. If you do ask family or friends to invest in your startup, make sure to have a written contract that states the amount invested and exactly what they get in return for their investment. Do not rely on verbal agreements only.

b. **Apply for Business Loans** (if needed) – You can apply for a business loan from banks, government backed loans or the Small Business Administration (SBA) loan programs. If applying for a loan, in most cases you will be required to provide a professional, detailed business plan.

SBA Loans – Loan programs designed for business owners who may have trouble qualifying for a traditional bank loan.
https://www.sba.gov/content/sba-loans

c. **Research Small Business Grants** - The federal government does not provide grants for starting a business. Federal grants are available to nonprofit and educational institutions. However, there are some very specialized federal grants in specific fields and industries such as medical/science research and environmental conservation. Also, there are some business grants available through nonprofit organizations and state/local programs. Usually these grants are for specialized businesses (women, minorities, veterans, etc.). If you have a good business plan, you will be better off seeking small business loans than government grants.

To read, *Government Grants for Small Businesses - Do you qualify?* Go to: https://www.sba.gov/blogs/government-grants-small-business-think-you-qualify

d. **Seek Venture Capital** – There are venture capitalists (investors who provide capital to startups or support small businesses that are rapidly growing for a return on their investment) that are looking for solid investments (for example - the investors on Shark Tank TV show are venture capitalists). However, seek this type of funding only if your business has the potential to achieve multi-million dollar sales/profits in a very short time.

For more information, contact:

National Venture Capital Association –
http://www.nvca.org
703-524-2549

Small Business Investment Alliance –
http://www.sbia.org
202-628-5055

Step 6:

Getting Organized

To succeed in business, to reach the top, an individual must know all it is possible to know about that business. – J. Paul Getty

First, decide if you will hire an accountant/CPA to handle your accounting or you may want to do it yourself with a small business accounting software such as Quickbooks. The goal is for the record keeping process to be as automated, accurate, and efficient as possible. The accounting process includes new orders (invoices, accounts receivable), paying bills (accounts payable), employees (payroll), state and federal tax forms filed and paid on time, reconciliation of all bank statements monthly, etc. When the process is effortless, you can concentrate your energy on building and growing your business.

Accounting Software :

Intuit Quickbooks – Accounting software for small business
http://quickbooks.intuit.com

Wave Software – Free accounting tools made specifically for entrepreneurs, freelancers, consultants and small businesses with 9 employees or less.
https://www.waveapps.com/accounting/

Step 7:

Location, Location, Location

Success in business requires training and discipline and hard work. But if you're not frightened by these things, the opportunities are just as great today as they ever were.
~David Rockefeller

A. Determine your Business Location

This will depend on your type of business. Will you start as a home-based business or will you need to look for office/retail space for your new business?

a. **Home-based Business** – If you decide to run a home-based business then it is very important to check city zoning requirements for your area.

b. **Leasing Office Space** – Prior to contacting a commercial realtor in your area, make a list of the features your business will need such as:

Size - how much square footage do you need?

Price -what is the maximum rent you can afford to pay? Try to negotiate the terms of the lease.

Location –choose a location wisely! Take your time and do the necessary research because your location can mean the difference between success and failure. Ask yourself these questions:

1. Is your target market (potential customers) located in this area?
2. What is the average earned income in this area?
3. Are there many competitors close to you? If yes, this can mean it's a premier location to attract new customers OR just the opposite in that it's over saturated and you will get no business. DO YOUR RESEARCH.

4. Will people be able to easily find you? Are you on a main road that can give you additional advertising and walk-in customers? Is there easy access to parking and public transportation?
5. What are the local, city and state zoning requirements for this area?

Once you sign a lease agreement for an office/retail space then you will need the necessary furniture, equipment, and supplies to furnish it and run your business.

B. Obtain Good, Reliable Suppliers (Wholesalers)

If you need to order inventory (retail, manufacturing), finding and forming trusted relationships with wholesalers takes time and research. Start by searching the Internet for wholesalers by product to help you find local and national suppliers. You can search wholesale directories such as **WholesaleCentral.com, WholesaleHUB.com** yellow pages, online associations, and trade shows/magazines (**Trade Show News Network – tsnn.com**). You can also contact specific brand manufacturers. They sometimes sell wholesale, but usually only in high volume but they may be able to refer you to a small business wholesaler.

Step 8:

Building a Team

I think it's safe to say that nothing runs itself by itself well. One must be committed to give full effort, full energy, full focus, full time to make a difference. Committed is a great word because it means that "I am willing to give it my best effort!" Being committed brings good things, resources and people to us.
~John Maxwell

In the beginning, the business owner usually is the main sales/service person doing multiple job tasks. However, you won't be able to do everything yourself so consider outsourcing to contractors, freelancers, and interns. Remember, trying to do everything yourself can take away from you working on growing the business. So later, in order to expand you will need to hire additional staff. With hiring employees there is payroll tax, state/federal forms, workers compensation insurance, unemployment taxes/insurance, benefit packages (optional), and other issues to consider. Your goal is to get a quality, good team in place. You will want to hire skilled employees that have a winning/positive attitude and share your values, goals and vision for the business.

Questions to consider when hiring an employee *[excerpt taken from* **Business Tool to Help You Increase and Grow Your Business** *(fiverr gig) by Violet James]* *http://www.fiverr.com/bizlifecoach*:

1. Is the employee fully competent and skilled for their job position?

2. Is the employee in the position that best uses his/her strengths?

3. Is the employee very clear about his/her job description and responsibilities?

4. Did I clarify what I expect from this employee?

5. Is the employee motivated? Does he/she have a winning/positive attitude? Does he/she

share the company's values, goals and vision for the business?

6. Is the new employee trained well?

7. Does he/she get along well with others and can work together as a team?

Step 9:

Developing a Business Identity

*To be successful, you have to have your heart
in your business, and your business in your
heart. – Sr. Thomas Watson*

Before you create a logo and your marketing
materials such as business cards, flyers,
postcards, letterhead, etc., you will want to
have a professional marketing plan. One of the
biggest mistakes you can make as a business
owner is to not have a marketing plan. This
step is so crucial especially when you are a
startup. You will want a marketing plan to
include the following:

- Research and understand your market
  and competition
- Identify your target market (customers)
- Create a compelling marketing
  message (slogan, elevator speech, etc.)
  to add to all marketing materials

- Create action plans to get new customers and
- Create action plans to retain existing customers

I put together a **Simple 5 Step Marketing Plan for Small Business Success** for only $5 (fiverr gig) that covers all of these essentials so there is no excuse not to have a marketing plan. *http://www.fiverr.com/bizlifecoach*

Step 10:

Opening Your Doors for Business

I'm convinced that about half of what separates the successful entrepreneurs from the non-successful ones is pure perseverance.
~Steve Jobs, Apple Inc. co-founder, chairman and CEO

Congratulations! All your hard labor has finally paid off. You are now ready to schedule an opening day for your business. This is the most exciting part. But first, you will want people to know that you are ready and open for business. You can have an Open House and invite as many people (family, friends, neighbors, potential customers, etc.) as possible. Offer special deals that day only. You can have food and entertainment to draw people in. You will want to also let the neighborhood and surrounding areas know you are open for business. You can print some professional flyers and distribute them door-to-door, place a local newspaper advertisement/ discounted coupon offer, send out local press releases, join the local Chambers of Commerce. They may support you with a ribbon cutting and advertisement. Get the word out any way you can- networking, cold-calling, etc.

After several months, take time to chart and record your progress in the following major key functional areas (sales and marketing, leadership and management, productivity, etc.). I put together an 84-item assessment checklist tool that covers all (7) of the major key areas - **_Business Tool to Help You Increase and Grow Your Business_** *(fiverr gig-* http://www.fiverr.com/bizlifecoach). This assessment tool will help you identify your strengths and weaknesses in these key areas so you can maximize growth and peak performance in your business.

You now have everything you need to start, grow and maintain a successful, thriving business! So, continue to work hard, stay positive and persistent. Never stop growing and learning and you will succeed!!

"The important thing is not being afraid to take a chance. Remember, the greatest failure is to not try."
~Debbie Fields., Mrs. Fields Bakeries founder

About the Author

Violet James, MSM is an entrepreneur, marketing and business manager, award-winning web designer, and artist. She has over 20 years experience in business consulting, marketing and management. She is the cofounder of NewDayCounseling.org and NewDayBooks.com. Violet has authored several best-selling books.

Connect with Violet James

It is my sincerest desire and hope that this book *How to Start a Business: Step-by-Step Guide* has made it simple and easy for you to start your own successful and thriving business. I would love to hear your testimonials and how you have been helped.

You can send your testimonials, feedback and comments to me at:

 maxpotential312@gmail.com

I encourage you to share your experience, and I would truly appreciate if you would write a review on Amazon.com

My author profile:
http://www.amazon.com/author/violetjames

Join our *Words of Inspiration* page and Friend us on Facebook:
http://www.facebook.com/WordsOfInspiration

Follow and connect with us on Twitter:
http://www.twitter.com/behappy4lifeNDC

Visit our *Be Your Best* blog (offers RSS):

http://www.newdaycounselingcenter.blogspot.com

LinkedIn:
http://www.linkedin.com/in/violetjames

Other Books & Resources by Violet James:

5 Simple Steps to Get Out of Debt: Live Debt-Free & Experience Financial Freedom

5 Step Marketing Plan for Small Business Success available in pdf format- Fiverr, Kindle format, Paperback and Audio

Startup 84 Item Checklist to Help You Grow Your Business - https://www.fiverr.com/bizlifecoach